My Silly Monster

By Luna Lark

BOOK BUNDLE

Download now

Meet Giggles, so bright, a chuckle in the air,
with Mom so calm, they make quite the pair.
"I'm so silly, watch me go!"
Laughter shared, a love they show.

Zippy zooms, all around,
Excitement bubbles, in leaps and bounds.
"I can't sit still, there's too much to see!"
Mom nods, "Explore, but stay close to me."

Bouncy, with jumps so high,
Reaching for clouds, in the sky.
"Let's play tag, and hide and seek!"
Mom smiles, "Your happiness, I'll always keep."

Frowny, red, with a scowl so deep,
Anger's flame, he struggles to keep.
"I'm so mad, I could roar!"
Mom's calm voice, "Let's talk, explore."

Frowny   Mom

Twisty, tangled, in a knot,
Things aren't working, feeling hot.
"It's not fair, I can't do it!"
Mom says, "Slow down, bit by bit."

Worrywart, pacing, a furrowed brow,
Imagining troubles, then and now.
"What if, what if," his constant plea,
Mom hugs, "Together, we'll see."

Tearful, blue, with a sniffle and sigh,
Sadness in heart, in the blink of an eye.
"I'm feeling down, don't know why,"
Mom's there, "I'm here, my sweet little guy."

Soothe, takes deep breaths, in and out,
Finding calm, without a doubt.
"Let's breathe deep," Mom guides the way,
Together, they find peace in play.

Calmly counts, one to five,
Slowing down, feeling alive.
"Count with me," Mom's voice a balm,
In their counting, finding calm.

Feel, notices how his body sings,
Listening closely, to what joy brings.
"Notice how you feel," Mom says with love,
Together, they fit, hand in glove.

Feel   Mom.

Chat, shares feelings, big and small,
With Mom to listen, standing tall.
"Let's talk it out," she gently insists,
In their conversation, love persists.

Stretch, in poses, finding space,
Yoga brings calm, at their own pace.
"Let's stretch together," Mom leads the way,
In every pose, their stress fades away.

stretch

Embrace, with arms wrapped tight,
Hugs from Mom, make everything right.
"A hug from me," she whispers, dear,
In her embrace, there's no fear.

BOOK BUNDLE

Download now

Made in United States
Troutdale, OR
02/19/2025

29119316R00019